Writing My Yoga

Writing
My Yoga

POEMS FOR PRESENCE

With much love to all here at Sylvan Lake — Be well! Fran Shaw 7/05

Fran Shaw

Indications Press
New York

With special thanks to my editor, Lillian Firestone.

Work Cited: Sri Aurobindo, *The Future Poetry,* Pondicherry: Sri Aurobindo Ashram, 1972.

Book Design by Yuko Uchikawa
Cover Art by R. David Shaw

Library of Congress Cataloging-in-Publication Data

Shaw, Fran Weber, 1947-
  Writing my yoga : poems for presence / Fran Shaw.
     p. cm.
   ISBN 0-9639100-2-7 (pbk. : alk. paper)
   1. Spiritual life--Poetry. I. Title.
   PS3619.H393W75 2004
   811'.54--dc22
                        2004006975

For my loving husband, R. David Shaw

CONTENTS

Writing My Yoga

FOREWORD

Every summer for eight years, I spent a week on retreat in the mountains with ninety people and a spiritual teacher. Although there wasn't much free time in the day's schedule, sometimes these poems would push their way into my notebooks. This book is a memoir of that time, in poetry and journal entries.

What began as a collection of poems became both the account of a journey and a book about writing. Each chapter begins with a moment that stands out for me, followed by three or four poems which came through at that time.

I've been teaching writing and making poems most of my life, but my understanding about composing them is different now. The act of listening for a poem changes me internally. It is a yoga.

There are poems—as haiku and Hindu poetics suggest— that give the savor of a moment in a way that rouses me and attracts me to an experience of another quality. But how to create such poems? What is the process? Who creates?

—Fran Shaw

1

THE PROCESS OF SEEING

Sitting on a mountainside on a warm July morning, listening to the hum of insects in the meadow.

A man wearing a hat and work gloves pushes a wheelbarrow up the path. On the veranda, two women set up a folding table, bring out fabric and scissors. In a few minutes, I guess, I'll pretend I can sew. At the moment, I have a sense of being under observation: from a balcony across the road, an old woman watches.

She reminds me of my grandmother. And that little girl scout, flowers in my hand, walking into the nursing home for the first time, seeing the elderly in wheelchairs and running scared out the door—

The clatter of dishes rises up from the dining hall. The cleanup after the meal. What was said at breakfast? Straining not to miss a word. Wanting to change according to some idea of how I should be.

But right now it's more like... looking at this hillside. I know I am listening. I know I'm in the process of seeing. It doesn't matter if the flowers are yellow or red.

Grandmother

She sits
stiffly in the asylum
of the afflicted,
her eyes

sunken,
her skin, powder
sifted with dust.
And milkless

breasts.
Her bones
have fallen out.
Frozen

moments
hang in jars
around her neck.
Her peace is

our disease:
our parent,
our terror.
We watch

the nimbus
radiate its death
around her head,
wait for

a sign.
We bring flowers
to turn away
her eyes.

Cleaning House

Closed-eye fantasies provide
confrontations with what's inside:
what you are, a clutter, a mess,
what you would be, meticulous.

"Who's going to clean up?"
I ask, thinking that I must
tuck in my shirt, dust
under the bed, and put

the trash in piles. Instead I
stuff my upholstered chassis.
On the wall, all the while,
Dalai Lama—lightning flashes!—
smiles broad smiles.

The Week in Review

Frustration
    Salvation
        Elation
Dissension
    Pretension
        Condescension
Hellion
    Rebellion
Coarse
    Force
        Source
            Remorse
Landing
    Understanding
Humility
    Responsibility

Tableaux

Silent, sunlit, still,
The clouds rest, tranquil.
The mountain peaks, alive,
Tableaux of air and light.
A presence felt, behind,
Shown in glowing skies,
In limbs touched by wind,
In every breathing thing.
My body on a chair,
No less than light divine,
A vapor in the air.

2

TALKING MACHINES

Once more, climbing the path up the mountain. With a nasty cold. Preoccupied here, of all places. Can I leave my baggage in the valley? Can I leave myself at the door?

I dread going to breakfast with everyone. I'm not ready for people yet. I don't fit in. I don't feel kind. And everyone will see my nastiness.

At breakfast, we are talking machines. Then, an announcement. No more discussions. Instead, sittings, music, and sacred dances which demand complete attention in each moment. And it opens me.

What is change? It's not that this or that characteristic becomes something else. It is that in a moment, I am radically changed, altogether changed, for that moment.

And I recognize it. The struggle to get rid of or go toward something is gone. No more dispersion. What a relief!

Whatever this energy is that passes through me, for the microseconds I live in it, my perception of people changes as well. I hear your words, yet I'm as interested in the light there in your eyes, the Life we share, the same in you as in me.

When I have an agenda for you—expectations, judgments—my state has contracted. I'm caught. The telling thought: If *you'd* shape up, *I'd* feel better. I avoid you because then I don't have to suffer my discomfort—my arrogance—

Blessed dis-ease! Something's not right with me, so I write. Going into receiving mode for the poem restores equilibrium—brings joy in being alive—and I am only glad when next I see you. How can that be? One toe in the ocean, and I am no longer at sea. We are here together for this, here in the current of life—the teacher in you, the teacher in me.

Face to Face

My house in shadow. The sun
comes out and warms the stones—
my bones—
I listen for direction.

The coarse word, the clenched fist—
one on one
with the wall of stone,
the sheer drop, I sit.

Nearby, a mountain spring
I hear but cannot see—
I am not free,
but still defend my suffering.

The Unspoken

If I could see the salt spray in your eyes,
you could talk to me any old way,
and there would be the splash and glitter
of a sunlit bay.

And each incoming wave brings ease,
and every skittering bird, a smile.
We'd watch the bubbles glint and pop—
for a while.

If I could hear the ocean in your voice,
you could say whatever you like,
and there would be the flash and tumble
of undulating light.

Sowing

Sewing in the sun
on the edge of a mountain
while the bell in the village tower
rings out the hour.

Pinning fabric, hands
know how to do,
see where to place the thread
and pull it through.

And what was thought difficult,
not so. Just here—
and the pines close by,
listening near—

Women peel onions
on a porch in the sun;
men with wheelbarrows
go up and down.

Sewing in the sun
on the edge of a mountain
while the bell in the village tower
rings out the hour.

3
THIS TASTE

After a week on the mountain, sitting on a bench by the lake.

I watch sailboats—everything—easily gliding by. Ducklings skirting the shore. Lilac fronds curving along the wall. Stone swans filled with red dahlias. The world in bloom. Like music—just let it come in.

The least minute when I'm quiet, looking out at the water, this taste again: I'm with my breathing, contained, at rest.

Here, a looking, a listening. My mind, a sensitive space. Interested in all my surroundings, including what's nearest: my body. From the top of my head to my seat on the chair to the soles of my feet—and subtle events—pulse, heartbeat. It's not what I see but what sees me.

A sensation wells up in my abdomen, heralding the first line of a poem. If something real comes, it orients me each time I read it.

Benchmark

A bench under a pine
by the lake with the snow-covered mountains.

Sun on the water: light cells in motion—
sparks of a larger ocean.

Is this how a moment expands
so time slows down?

Listening in the cool air
under a sliver of morning moon—

Is this the new season?

All the Things

All the things I tell myself—

Ripples, ripples,
and the waters wash through.

All the things I think are true—

The lake surface quivers
with falling raindrops.

All the times not getting what I want—

Reflected trees blurring:
the trees are doubled.

All at once to feel the touch—

The sky fills the lake
from shore to shore.

Waterfall

From a source I cannot see
    falls the airy stream,
filaments pulsating light
    along rock walls.
Here air and water mingle
    in the downward rush
from snowy ledge to vapor
    disappearing in the trees.
So thin and fine a plume,
    blending with the shadows,
it can go unnoticed among the stones.
    Yet the light catches the drops
and spills tenderness into all
    who, listening behind the sound,
stand still a moment in the flow.

4

ELECTIVE HUMILIATION

Lugging my bags on the long dirt road. Why come to the mountain and put myself in conditions of discomfort? What do I expect? To meet my Self.

I'm the first one in the door. The house is empty but I fill it with myself, as the Buddhists say. I watch the arrivals. Who's that strutting around like he knows it all? Unlike him, I don't know much. (Oh, maybe a little something.)

That evening I'm asked to speak in front of ninety people. Heart pounding. Trying not to show I'm nervous. Inner attention feels thready. My voice, so in earnest, and then, suddenly, along with the words, I hear the lie in them, recognize the attitude behind—can everybody see?—

Look who thinks she's Somebody.

Afterward, I race around asking, "Was it all right?" I need comfort. I need spin! People are so kind. These same people.

I get ready for bed. I just want to go to sleep. I'm a fake. An idiot. And now we all know. In bed at night, I cry under the covers.

Look who thinks she's Nobody.

And watch myself cry—how odd—to feel the wetness of every tear roll down my cheeks. To watch the event as if seen from outside—a body crying—releasing all that's been bottled up unawares. Such a strain, holding up a front, protecting… what? Self-image. *You mean, I don't have to live in that one little room any more?* A fresh burst of tears—of gratitude.

The next morning, I wake up glad to be here with everyone. No more hiding. No more pretending. If you see through me—good—maybe I can, too. Are we not alike in this? At any moment, ego either dominates or serves.

Exposure brings a state which is appreciated. I write a poem to record for myself what it feels like to wish only to let the seeing continue.

Ruffled Feathers

Perched upon an attitude
of "I know-and-you-don't,"
my lark will hear her song as best—
until, one day, she won't.

Then sorry tears give way to bits
of plumage on the ground,
and mute even my mockingbird;
my peacock makes no sound.

And now a certain stillness
that rustles in the leaves
can thread a silken tendril
from heart to heart with ease

And bring translucent skies of blue
which may not long remain—
though many more reminding tears
may light the way again.

Out of the Corner

Out of the corner of my eye,
a demi-moon, a butterfly;
and yet, an empty sky.

A bumblebee, a little lie,
a passing cloud, a dream gone by;
an empty sky.

Into silence, every sigh;
no more you, no more I.
Now, an empty sky.

Caterpillar Thoughts

A buzzing in the summer grass,
like chatter in the brain,
contains within the silent wings
of butterflies unchained.

What truth is hid in buzzing brains?
What insect of delight?
Between the one that comes and goes,
what space, what force, what light?

Clearing the Rains

When the fog disappears from the meadow
with a fine mist on the wing,
softly the wind stirs the pine boughs;
softly the morning can sing.

All life comes alive in the sunlight,
the rocks no less fine than the air;
the clouds roll away in their own time
the moment we see what we share.

This new way to live with each other,
this shining which nothing can mar,
will give us a gift without measure:
the freedom to be who we are.

5
SIDE ALLEYS

In a spa town for a day after a week on the mountain. Taking the ski lift with the summer hikers.

Chocolate brown cows graze in the meadow.

I sit on the terrace of an alpine restaurant. Full of energy. Everywhere, a poem. Even that concrete wall I have to write about! I spill over into my notebook. Some lines vibrational, some intellectual.

Do I notice when poetic feeling carries me down the side alley of poeticizing? Impressions are no longer actively received in awareness. In their place: cleverness, Ideas. A shift has occurred: in the afterglow of the retreat, I'm more eager to be eloquent than to *be*. I write, *"The mind in focus, the heart opens."* Simple truth? Or showing off? Something smells....

A Glossary of Terms for the "Esoteric" Poet

Foot—the small metrical unit that goes into a mouth full of pronouncements

Heroic couplet—bravely trying to sum up the nature of reality in two lines

Hyperbole—exaggerating every detail; after all, it must be Important because it's happening to me

Pathetic fallacy—the false, pathetic, inflated notion of my status, as in the line, *"All nature wept when Fran's car was repossessed"*

Personification—becoming a person *IF* only I can take a vacation from everything I think, feel, and believe

Hikers, please don't interrupt me with your questions. Can't you see? I'm Writing!—

The ringing of cow bells...

Lifts my glib head from the page. *Where am I?*

And then: the mountains. Curving into and out of one another. The sunlight. My pores open to it. Because there is something so compelling in the silence of a hundred mountain peaks.

The Lift

Waiting in the sky
to descend,
waiting with sunny peaks
where every detail speaks
to descend,
into worries, into dreams,
covered up again,
while inside, at the same time—
to ascend
into forests
into caves,
to ascend
into turquoise pools,
to ascend,
ever to arrive.
And yet—
and here's the lift—
in both, to be alive.

Am I?

The eyes through which the mountain sees
   everything that lives and breathes;
a pore of earth through which life moves
   a stone to moss, a bud to bloom;
the earth's ears, the human hum,
   the wide silence everywhere sung;
a line of footprints by the sea—
   am I are you is she are we?

Observation Point

The stone crevasse
   receives the sun.
The mountain pass
   receives the sun.
The glacial lake
   receives the sun.
The upturned face
   receives the sun.
Peak upon peak
   receives the sun
Into the deep
   listening core,
Without a thought,
   without a word—
Though I receive,
   Be here. Stay more.

6

LIKE A BALL IN PLAY

Ice storm. Winter in Vermont. Longing for summer's heights.

A lump on a couch. Obsessing about a problem. Filled with notions of how I should be. My attention, like a ball in play.

Hands cutting a grapefruit. Cleaning the counter. My thoughts on automatic pilot. Hands in water washing dishes. Take a nap?

Go out. Hike up the old ski trail.

With the first steps: snow crystals shine in the sun. Cold air. Cold hands. Inside my gloves, I curl my fingers into my palms.

There are pockets under the trail where my leg drops through into snow up to the knee. I must feel my way with each footfall.

So beautiful, the soft curves the snow makes of slope and bush. Nature, the awakener. Attracting the interest to the larger world always here. An unlimited dimension?

Yearning for a certain state becomes yielding to what is.

As It Is

Bare winter trees, a thicket, stripped.
Yet not one leaf is missed
where limbs thread the air
and the light appears.

Iced-over stream, frozen, stopped.
Yet not one drop resists
where slippery shadows show
beneath the ice, the flow.

Beneath the hard silver,
the gold gently quivers.

Snow Gems

All winter, waiting for the sky to open,
I walk the mountain path to find the means.
I must, I should, I can't—although unspoken—
Snow burdens weighing down the evergreens.
And yet the trees aren't bare but even budding:
Observe the birches splayed along the heights.
The hills, whose snowy sinews bear close study,
Display a fine-spun net of diamond lights.
And everywhere the forest trail is gleaming
With bursts of crystal keeping us on course;
A world more radiant than we ever dreamed of,
Where each distress but leads us to the source;
And latticed shadows on the forest floor
Compel our grateful gaze a moment more.

Gently, Gently

Gently, gently…
"Be with the difficulty."

Walk with it—

Where the air is lit
with snow dust.

Keep watch with it—

While birches gather
on the hill.

Allow it—can I?—

Here the stream
goes underground.

A distant mountain calls
across the ages.

A brown leaf dances
on the snow.

The tiniest twig
Reveals itself.

7

WHEN ONE DOOR CLOSES

After a quarter of a century together, our small group for waking up is breaking up. I don't know what's going on.

I had come to the group as a young woman with high expectations. My teachers were wonderful. I idolized them.

Decades later, the fallout from personal conflicts and illness kept hidden behind the scenes seeps into our meetings. The atmosphere deteriorates into arguing. The one time I speak up I'm told if I don't like it, I can go elsewhere. A scary thought.

Disillusionment sets in. I try to see my blind egoism in all this, understand what others are going through. A homeopathic doctor treats me for nerve pain in my back. I look up the remedy. What's it for? The words come as a shock: "suppressed rage."

Go on as before? I'd have to play the Good Student again. I can't place myself in someone else's hands any more. I have to know for myself who I am.

What does it take for me stand on my own? No one to follow. Something must come from me. Can I trust what's in me, and that it can show me the path to it?

But I'm so used to looking for help from outside. Who will help me now?

The sun has set. I step out onto the frozen lake and listen.

The Fight

Listening
   or bristling?

Loving
   or shoving?

The soul
   or control?

Bless
   or suppress?

Forgive
   or relive?

To flee
   or to be?

To the Glacier

Frozen folds
of earth and snow
seem unmoved,
and yet, they flow—

Flow through me here
so I feel what we are,
O, silver mountain,
sky-touched fountain.

Guru on Ice

The slippery mirror of a frozen lake
    reflects a jet pursuing sunset,
        trailing signatures and faces,
          flying me into a blaze
Of white. What now—Whose wings?—
    A gull comes eyeing, tunes to my seeking,
      tips a wing in greeting:
        That is the teaching.

8

BOTH NATURES

A group of us climbs the mountain at sunrise and sings by the lake. So corny but… it's just so BIG out today!

We walk along aqua-white waters of glacial streams. Past waterfalls, through forests. I stop on a bridge to watch the tall grasses stirring—something so delicate in the vibration, I feel it inside.

"Come look over here," my artist friend calls to me. On the ground under a tree, the petticoat of a wood nymph: a three-foot-wide orange mushroom with ruffled yellow edges. At every turn, the aliveness in these woods makes me wish only to be conscious in this sacred valley.

Later, we walk back into town. Not a thought in my head. No one has felt the impulse to say anything for an hour, the air is so filled with silence. And then, through an open door, the sound of a man's voice… pierces the heart! Human being! A life here in this house. In faces, that same quality as in the tall grasses. A tender life in others, seen only when I am here.

Is this what's meant by the heart closing and opening? I must live closed because I opened for a few seconds and the world is different. No judgments. A quality pouring through that compels attention—we are made for love—for a flowing through into the world.

All the World

Where all the world is filled with light
    And we are filled—and light as air,
Transparent, just a wisp of life
    Walking here and looking there,
Breathed by earth and sun and stars,
    We bathe in flowing mountain streams,
Gliding with the clouds and wind,
    Free of longing, free of dreams.

Unison

Over root-tangled steps,
    loose rock underfoot,

a strand of hikers,
    all of one mind,

threads its way
    across spilt stone

up where snow fields
    outshine the sun:

one earth, one heart,
    one voice—
        one.

At the Café

Walking for hours,
amid rock walls and waterfalls,
when on the path back to town

Seeing people again.
Going past an open door—
inside, a man whistling—

At the café,
the woman laughing,
the man nodding.

Then you asked me,
and I could not speak.

9

NOT OUR USUAL PLANET

Back home from the mountain. Feet go numb in the icy Atlantic. The vista: flat, wide, everywhere moving.

I stand with my notebook in hand waiting to write. People on the beach look at me as they walk by. I wish the beach were empty. I'm more hermit than this crab. Do my surroundings have to be a certain way so I can be a certain way? Do I need the beach to be quiet and empty for me to… be?

A few feet away on the sand, there's a large grey gull also looking out to sea. I notice I'm standing just as still and at exactly the same angle as the gull. Suddenly, we are gulls together.

An old man, as he walks by, puts his hands together as in prayer and says, "Meditate." Whoa! That never happened before. I put away my notebook. Don't write now. Meditate.

The gull walks. I walk. Bodies in motion in the whoosh of waves.

Everywhere the Light

Everywhere the light touches
the rolling ocean,
Earth shines silver,
spirals in motion.

Everywhere the wind touches,
white foam glides,
line upon line,
with such devotion.

Everywhere, the light touches
the rolling ocean.
Everywhere the breath touches,
the path opens.

Sea Change

Two gulls step up to breakfast:
a live crab on its back.
I turn it over, gently nudge it
seaward from the flats.
No such concern for passers-by.
I hide under my hat.
The nosy looks, the scrutiny—
I just can't get past that.

Until this moment, beach astir—
Who's swimming in the sea?
Buoyant with the seals, my heart
is changed—but not by me.
Who smiles now at strangers?
Aren't they beautiful? Come see!

Stars Above, Stars Below

Full moon
Empty beach

Whole sky
Within reach

Silver flecks
Stars in sand

Whose heart?
Whose hand?

How to Quiet the Mind

Go wide,
says the ocean
says the sky

Alive,
say the trees
say the tides

Align,
say the stars
say the wise

And fly,
says the light
winging by.

10

ALWAYS, ONLY THE BEGINNING

The last day of the last summer on the mountain. The chalet, sold.

I'm on my bed in the women's dorm. The room is empty. The only sound, my breathing. Here I sit, in the current of life. In its tempo. Not against anything, not pushing. Moving through the world aware of that which animates my body. I do not know what it is, but it lights me up. Everything is new.

Who am I? The question has been posed. The best of questions because it's unanswerable. Except—to look. To appear. I try to carry the question, ask it when I am too much concentrated on my concerns. *Who am I,* here in this breathing body, looking out of these eyes.

Wake up to write. Write to wake up. Becoming the blank page. Even though words express a state of mind, sometimes waiting silently for them brings a drop of reality.

When words feel true, who is speaking? *Who...?*

Mountain Breathing

mountain breathing
only breathing
mountain breathing
bright with being
human being
mountain breathing

In the Garden

Cool shade
Hot sun
In the garden
Work's begun

Not mine and not yours
But ours to know
We just listen in
Sensing the flow

Now I come closer
Now I exist
I appear in my face
I gently persist

Nothing to gain
Nothing to lose
Open to life
Nothing to choose

Curving Into View

A cloud
clings to the summit.

Every turn of the trail,
the slippery moraine—

Remember, remember,
why you're here—calling,

You are near
You can be.

Follow the hidden river
now curving into view,

carrying us lightly
along the precipice.

At the top of the world
—silence—

Can it be so?

Interior skies endlessly
opening?

Even As We Are

Branches bent low by ice.
With each gust, the swirls
of snow along the rise
lift up like unseen energies
made visible by wind.
Each ice-bound limb
bears glints of loving worlds
we can't recall—but ah! this light
so vivifies the eye
that even as we are we rise
with mists of snow becoming sky.

AFTERWORD: WRITING YOUR YOGA

I remember reading in college that poems can come from active awareness to "capture that vibrating thing," and that the poet can aspire to be a "transcribing agent": "The use of keeping the consciousness uplifted is that it then remains ready for the flow from above when that comes" (Sri Aurobindo, *The Future Poetry,* 1972, p. 299).

Maybe you're experimenting in this mode. For me, the sole aim is to be alert in this place each instant. There's a moment when watching and listening is felt to be more important than whether or not a poem comes. That's when I pick up the pen. Enjoy!

How to Write Your Yoga Poem

1. Sit in a favorite place, preferably outdoors.
2. *Breathe* in, breathe out, in full awareness.
3. *Listen* to all the sounds… or for the silence behind them.
4. *Look* deeply at anything, while aware of your peripheral vision.
5. Write phrases and images describing this place in this moment.

...And then try any of these variations:

—Say out loud your burning question today,
   and look to this landscape for the answer;
   write whatever comes.

—Place a word or two on the page, as a
   springboard, such as

> Now
> If
> Along the
> All
> Out of
> With these

—Turn on your ipod or walkman, and let classical
   music merge with this place to inspire a poem.
   (Try the second movement of Beethoven's *Sixth*.)

—Close your eyes for a few moments and listen;
   open your eyes and write down the *first*
   thing that you see. Keep writing.

—Describe only what you see, hear, smell,
   taste, and touch, one impression per line,
   in groups of three.

May you fill the world with poems.

FRAN WEBER SHAW, Ph.D., is the author of
50 Ways to Help You Write, book reviews, articles,
textbooks, and the *Write It Up* video course.
A Danforth Fellow and a Woodrow Wilson
Fellow, and winner of two national awards for
poetry, she is Associate Professor of English at
the University of Connecticut at Stamford.
Recipient of the Amy Loveman Poetry Prize,
she is a graduate of Barnard College, Stanford
University, and the Union Institute, and has
been guiding writing workshops across the
country for over twenty years.